ALLEN COUNTY PUBLIC LIBRARY

3 1833 05294 0621

D0883393

A Robbie Reader

A Robbie Reader

Ultra Running with Scott Jurek

Jim Whiting

Mitchell Lane
PUBLISHERS

P.O. Box 196
Hockessin, Delaware 19707
Visit us on the web: www.mitchelllane.com
Comments? email us: mitchelllane@mitchelllane.com

Mitchell Lane PUBLISHERS

Copyright © 2007 by Mitchell Lane Publishers. All rights reserved. No part of this book may be reproduced without written permission from the publisher. Printed and bound in the United States of America.

Printing   1   2   3   4   5   6   7   8   9

Extreme Sports
Extreme Cycling with Dale Homes
Extreme Skateboarding with Paul Rodriguez
Ride the Giant Waves with Garrett McNamara
Ultra Running with Scott Jurek

Library of Congress Cataloging-in-Publication Data
Whiting, Jim, 1943-.
    Ultra running with Scott Jurek / by Jim Whiting.
        p. cm. — (A Robbie reader. Extreme sports)
    Includes bibliographical references and index.
    ISBN 1-58415-484-5 (library bound)
    1. Jurek, Scott, 1973– 2. Runners (Sports) — United States — Biography. 3. Marathon running — Juvenile literature. I. Title. II. Series.
        GV1061.15.J874W485 2006
        796.42092 — dc22
                                                                2006006099
                                                        ISBN-13: 9781584154846
ISBN-10: 1-58415-484-5

ABOUT THE AUTHOR: Jim Whiting has been a journalist, writer, editor, and photographer for more than 30 years. He has written and edited about 200 nonfiction children's books. His subjects range from authors to zoologists and include contemporary pop icons and classical musicians, saints and scientists, emperors and explorers. Representative titles include *The Life and Times of Franz Liszt, The Life and Times of Julius Caesar, Charles Schulz,* and *Juan Ponce de Leon.*

Other career highlights are a lengthy stint publishing *Northwest Runner,* the first piece of original fiction to appear in *Runners World* magazine, hundreds of descriptions and venue photographs for America Online, sports editor for the *Bainbridge Island Review,* and acting as the official photographer for the Antarctica Marathon. He lives in Washington state with his wife and two teenage sons.

PHOTO CREDITS: Cover, pp. 1, 3, 4 — Luis Escobar; p. 7 — Ben Furtado; pp. 8 — Luis Escobar; p. 10 — Scott Jurek; pp. 12, 14 — Luis Escobar; p. 16 — Ben Furtado; p. 17, 18, 20, 21 — Luis Escobar; p. 22 — Jim Whiting; p. 24 — Luis Escobar; p. 25 — Jim Whiting; p. 27 — Ben Furtado; p. 28 — Luis Escobar

PUBLISHER'S NOTE: This book is based on personal interviews with Scott Jurek conducted by author Jim Whiting in January 2006. It has been approved for print by Scott Jurek. However, Mr. Jurek received no remuneration for this project and therefore the book should not be considered endorsed or authorized by him. While every possible effort has been made to ensure accuracy, the publisher will not assume liability for damages caused by any inaccuracies in the data.

DISCLAIMER: The sport of ultramarathoning should not be attempted without extensive training, experience, and professional assistance. This is both a high-risk and dangerous sport and may result in serious injury and may even cause death. Always consult with a trained professional before trying any new sport. Mitchell Lane Publishers shall not be held liable for any injuries to or damages caused by individuals attempting this sport. *Always Put Safety First.*

TABLE OF CONTENTS

*Words in **bold type** can be found in the glossary.

Scott Jurek strides easily along Robinson Flat, part of the Western States 100-Mile Endurance Run. The race is held in the Sierra Nevada in California. Robinson Flat is about 24 miles into the race.

A VERY DIFFICULT RACE

Scott Jurek was more than one-third of the way through the race. He was hot and tired, with his legs especially weary—and he was several miles behind the leader. Many people would have been tempted to quit. Not Scott.

He was competing in the Badwater **Ultramarathon** (UL-truh MAYR-uh-thon). A marathon is a footrace of 26.2 miles. Many big cities throughout the world host marathons. Thousands of people enter them.

An ultramarathon is longer than a marathon. At 135 miles long, the Badwater

Ultramarathon is like running five marathons back to back. It begins at 10:00 A.M. in Death Valley, California. At the start of the race, the temperature is often already 115 degrees. It is even hotter on the **asphalt** (AS-falt) road. At night the temperature drops only into the 90s. The course includes two mountain passes. Each one is nearly a mile high. The last 13 miles are all uphill. The finish line is halfway up Mount Whitney, the highest mountain in the continental United States.

Being so far behind wasn't Scott's only problem. His stomach was upset. He threw up at the 75-mile mark. Another time he was so tired that he wanted to sleep. He did—for five minutes.

Scott told himself, *I can get through this.* He pushed himself forward and won the race, giving a triumphant yell as he crossed the line. He was two hours ahead of the next racer. He also set a course record of 24 hours and 36 minutes. He ran at an average of less than 11 minutes per mile.

In the 2003 Western States 100, Scott finished more than an hour ahead of the second-place runner. It was his sixth straight win at Western States.

What was even more remarkable was that he had won a very difficult 100-mile race just two weeks before. Most people need months to recover from running such a hard race.

Scott Jurek is probably the best ultramarathon runner in the United States. Yet he didn't like running when he was growing up.

Scott smiles the morning after the 2006 Leona Divide 50-Mile Run. The race is held in the mountains in southern California. He has won the event four times.

A CHALLENGING CHILDHOOD

Scott Jurek was born on October 26, 1973, in Proctor, Minnesota. His father, Gordon, works as a heating and air-conditioning engineer. His mother, Lynn, was a home economics teacher. Then she became a homemaker.

Scott has a sister, Angela, who is two years younger. His brother, Greg, is five years younger. The Jurek children grew up in a rural area. Scott liked to make trails and build forts in the woods. His family did a lot of hunting, fishing, and camping. Scott also enjoyed Little League baseball, soccer, and basketball. He would sometimes run, but he wasn't interested in running as a sport.

While Scott (kneeling) was attending Proctor High School, he became a very good cross country skier. His younger brother, Greg, behind him, also played school sports.

Scott had to do many chores. He split and stacked wood and cut the grass. When he was about ten, his work became even harder. His mother was diagnosed with **multiple sclerosis** (MUL-tih-pul skler-OH-sis). It became difficult for her to walk. Eventually she was confined to a wheelchair. Today she is in a nursing home.

Scott, Angela, and Greg had to do all the things their mother usually did, such as keep the

3 1833 05294 0621

house clean and do the laundry. There wasn't much time to play with friends.

Many youngsters would have whined. Not Scott. "Growing up the way we did gave us a lot of self-confidence," he says. "We learned how to be independent and challenge ourselves." He would use these lessons later in life. They are just some of the many discoveries that helped to form him into the man he is today.

His mother's illness inspired his future career. A **physical therapist** (FIH-zih-kul THAYR-uh-pist) took care of her, helping her move her body. The movement eased Lynn's suffering. Scott was impressed. He wanted to help people the same way.

In high school, Scott began cross-country ski racing. He became very good at the sport. He represented the Midwest in a Junior Olympics competition in 1992. He ran a little bit, but that was only to help get in shape. Even during the summer, he preferred to **roller ski** than to run.

That all changed one hot day in 1994.

Scott breezes along the course of the Copper Canyon Run in March 2006. The race is held in the Sierra Madre in Mexico. It features several runners from the legendary Tarahumara Indian tribe. A century ago, the Tarahumara hunted deer by running after them until the deer dropped from exhaustion.

CHAPTER
THREE

A Robbie Reader

FINDING HIS TALENT

When Scott was about 20 years old, a friend named Dusty Olson asked him to run with him in a 50-mile race. Scott was already training for a marathon, so he added some long trail runs. Scott came in second. His friend was third.

Scott was exhausted. The air was 88 degrees and very **humid.** He told himself that "no way" would he ever run such a long race again.

He soon reconsidered. *I'm pretty good at this,* he told himself. "I started to really enjoy training."

He returned to the race for the next four years. He won three times.

The year 1994 was significant for another reason. He met his future wife, Leah. They were married in 1996. She has always been very supportive of his running. When Scott competes in ultramarathons, he needs a crew of several people to help out. Leah acts as the crew chief.

Scott and his wife, Leah, share a happy moment after the Leona Divide race in 2006. Both Scott and Leah are very careful to eat a healthy diet. It is ironic that they met at a fast food restaurant.

In 1999, he and Leah made a big decision. Scott had received his physical therapy degree the previous year. Now he took a physical therapy job with a health company in Seattle, Washington.

That same year he entered the Western States 100, the most famous ultramarathon in the United States. It covers 100 miles on a very rugged mountain trail in California's Sierra Nevada. The race takes place in late June, when the temperature can be either more than 100 degrees or else very cold. Some years there is even snow. One runner said that he started this race in the best shape of his life and finished in the worst shape. To compete, people have to be very strong mentally as well as physically.

Before the race, Scott was talking about how he would win. His opponents were astonished. They hadn't heard of him. They knew he had never run the course before. They thought he was being cocky. He wasn't.

Scott is very self-confident. He doesn't brag about his accomplishments. He lets his feet do the talking for him. They talk very well. He led the race from start to finish.

The race was more difficult the following year. Scott slipped back into fourth place. The leaders were pulling away from him. Somehow

Scott leads several other runners during the Western States 100. This high in the mountains, there is still snow, even though it is June.

Scott wears special protective clothing for the Badwater Ultramarathon. The hat has pockets for ice to cool his head. Ice bandanas cool his neck, back, and chest. The light-colored shirt and pants reflect the sun and decrease its heat.

he managed to dig deep inside himself to find the strength to win again.

In 2001, he sprained his ankle early in the race. In 2002, he was very sick a month before the race and missed valuable training time. He still won both times. That set a record: No one had ever won the race four times in a row.

Scott demonstrates stretching techniques for a group of people at a workshop on the Western States Trail. He likes to help other people do well in their running.

BRANCHING OUT

In 2003, Scott, who likes to share his knowledge, made several important changes. He started his own physical therapy business; he established running camps; and he began coaching other runners.

All these projects didn't seem to slow him down. He won Western States again. The following year he set a course record when he covered the 100 miles in 15 hours, 36 minutes, and 27 seconds. No one else was in sight when Scott finished. He rolled across the line six times to signify his six victories.

He wasn't boasting or trying to show anyone up. "I like to do something different at the finish," he says. "I want to show people that I'm not barely crawling in."

He also likes to whoop and holler while he's running. "It energizes me," he says. "Ultramarathoning isn't a super-exciting **spectator sport.** I try to liven it up a little."

Scott (center) lets out a big yell at the start of the 2004 Western States 100. To his left (in the white jersey) is Tim Twietmeyer, who won the race five times in the 1990s.

In 2005, he was about an hour slower than his record time, but there was a good reason. There was a lot of snow on the course.

Some people compare Scott to cyclist Lance Armstrong. The two men both won the most famous event in their sport seven straight times. Both men decided not to try for eight straight.

There is a big difference between the two. Armstrong retired from competitive racing, but Scott didn't. At age 33, he wanted to do other races. "I needed a break in my pattern," he said.

Scott probably will return to Western States. Most ultra runners don't hit their peak until their late 30s or even 40s. "I'm young for my sport," he said in 2006. "I have a lot of years ahead of me."

Scott catches up on some paperwork in his office in Seattle. Because of his many activities, he has to be very efficient with his time. A friend gave him the Japanese drawing on the wall. It is about the importance of inner drive and perseverance.

LOOKING FOR NEW CHALLENGES

Scott's personality is one reason for his success. He is very relaxed and easygoing. He likes being with people, and he supports everyone else in his races. He doesn't leave until everyone has finished.

Another reason is his diet. He is a **vegan** (VEE-gun). He doesn't eat meat or any animal products, such as milk or eggs. He won't touch junk food. "It's part of my training, to put quality food in my body," he says. He likes to spend time in the kitchen. He uses a blender to make fresh vegetable juice and other nutritious food.

Scott prepares nutritious blended snacks for participants at his Western States Trail Camp. People travel from all over the country to attend.

His diet helps him maintain his weight of 165 pounds. He is six feet, two inches tall.

Most weekdays he runs for 45 to 75 minutes. On the weekends he normally does back-to-back six-hour runs. For the long runs, he usually goes to one of the wilderness areas near Seattle. Because he doesn't own a car, he takes the bus to and from his starting point. He also stretches and does yoga.

While big city marathons pay a lot of prize money, ultramarathons usually don't pay anything. The prize for Western States, for example, is a bronze statue of a cougar. It weighs more than 30 pounds.

In fact, Scott lost money at the beginning of his ultramarathon career. Competing is still expensive. He has to pay for transportation and housing. Western States costs about $2,000.

Scott holds one of the trophies he has won at the Western States 100. He stands in front of an inspirational poster that features him.

Badwater is even more expensive. He needs to bring more support people and rent two vans. It costs him more than $4,000.

Fortunately, several fitness companies sponsor Scott. Some provide him with direct financial support. Others supply him with their products. That saves Scott a lot of money. For example, a shoe company gives him free shoes. He uses more than twenty pairs every year.

It also helps that he and Leah, who is a **massage therapist,** have jobs that pay well. They see patients three or four days a week, then they take an office day to catch up on paperwork. Their running camps, consulting, and coaching add to the amount of records they have to keep. They also travel frequently. Because they do so many things, they have to be very well organized. It helps that they don't spend time watching television.

Why does Scott run so much?

The main reason is that it's fun. "I've always told myself if I'm not having fun with ultramarathon

Scott greets the fans as he finishes the Western States 100. The race starts at 5:00 A.M., and he finishes around 9:00 P.M. Yet he stays until 11:00 the following morning so he can greet all the other finishers.

racing and competitive racing, I just won't do it," Scott said.

Another reason is satisfaction. When he finished Badwater, Scott said it felt like fireworks going off. "You feel on top of the world," he said.

Because he likes to run trails, Scott knows the importance of the natural world. "We have to take care of the environment," he says.

Scott's running has taught him not to place limits on himself. He says that in sports or in school, people don't know what they're capable of until they try. "Keep an open mind," he emphasizes. "Don't be afraid to explore new things."

Scott continues to set many challenges for himself. He wants to break 24 hours in the Badwater race. He wants to run ultramarathons in Europe. He wants to see how far he can run in 24 hours.

Scott doesn't think he will ever run out of challenges. When he finished Badwater, he said, "There's something there in the outside world and in myself that's yet to be discovered, that I want to find."

For Scott Jurek, life is a continual process of discovery.

CHRONOLOGY

1973   Scott is born on October 26 in Minnesota.

1984   Scott's mother becomes seriously ill with multiple sclerosis.

1992   Scott graduates from Proctor High School.

1994   Scott enters his first ultramarathon race and finishes second.

1996   Scott marries Leah.

1998   Scott obtains his physical therapy degree from the College of St. Scholastica in Minnesota.

1999   Scott and Leah move to Seattle, Washington; Scott wins Western States 100 for the first time.

2000   Scott defends his title at Western States.

2003   Scott opens his own physical therapy business; he wins Western States 100 for the fifth time.

2004   Scott sets a course record at Western States.

2005   Scott wins Western States for the seventh time. He wins Badwater Ultramarathon two weeks later in a record-breaking 24 hours and 36 minutes.

2006   Scott enters races in Europe. He wins the Badwater Ultramarathon again, despite flash floods and 120 degree weather.

FIND OUT MORE

Books

Hayhurst, Chris. *Ultra Marathon Running*. New York: Rosen Publishing Group, 2001.

Manley, Claudia B. *Competitive Track and Field for Girls*. New York: Rosen Publishing Group, 2001.

Parker, Steve. *Running a Race*. New York: Franklin Watts, 1991.

Savage, Jeff. *Working Out: Running*. Parsippany, New Jersey: Crestwood House, 1995.

Works Consulted

This book is based on the author's personal interview with Scott Jurek on January 20, 2006.

2006 Kiehl's Badwater Ultramarathon Race Magazine
http://www.adventurecorps.com/downloads/

Badwater Ultramarathon
http://www.badwater.com/index.html

Sabalow, Ryan. "Jurek Sets New Course Record at Badwater Ultramarathon," *Auburn Journal,* July 14, 2005.
http://www.coolrunning.com/engine/3/3_6/jurek-sets-new-course-rec.shtml

On the Internet

For more information about Scott's running camps
http://www.beyond-running.com

For more information about Scott
http://www.scottjurek.com

KidsRunning.com
http://www.kidsrunning.com

Way Cool Running Kid's Page
http://www.waycoolrunning.com

GLOSSARY

asphalt   (AS-falt)—a substance similar to tar that is used for paving roads.

humid   (HYOO-mid)—having a great deal of moisture.

massage therapist   (muh-SAJ THAYR-uh-pist)—a person who rubs people's muscle tissue to help them recover from injuries or stress.

multiple sclerosis   (MUL-tih-pul skler-OH-sis)—a disease in which people gradually lose control over their muscles.

physical therapist   (FIH-zih-kul THAYR-uh-pist)—a person who uses specialized treatments such as simple exercises to help people recover from serious illness or injuries.

roller ski   a sport using inline skates instead of skis to go quickly across country; generally done on flat surfaces.

spectator sport   (SPEK-tay-tur SPORT)—a sport that people enjoy watching rather than participating directly themselves, such as baseball, football, and basketball.

ultramarathon   (UL-truh MAYR-uh-thon)—a footrace that covers more ground than a regular marathon of 26.2 miles. Most ultramarathons are at least 50 miles long.

vegan   (VEE-gun)—a person whose diet consists of fruits, vegetables, nuts, and grains but no meat or animal products (such as eggs, milk, or cheese).

INDEX